# The Brontë Parsonage

Published by The Council of the Brontë Society

# Contents

First published by The Council of The Brontë Society in April 1962

©The Brontë Society

Revised by Mark R. D. Seaward and Vanessa A. Hinton in May 1978

Reprinted with revisions in 1984 and 1986

Designed by Anthony B. Ainley

Printed by Sunstreet Printing Works (Keighley) Ltd.

Front cover photograph by Simon Warner, Stanbury

Inside cover illustrations (The Dining Room and Rev. P. Bronté's Study) by Simon Warner, Stanbury

All photographs ©The Incorporated Bronté Society

Page  3    The Story of the Brontës
           SIR LINTON ANDREWS

     11    Chronology
           JULIET R. V. BARKER

     15    The Novels of the Brontës
           PHYLLIS BENTLEY

     21    The Brontës as Poets
           WILFRED ROWLAND CHILDE

     27    The Bronté Parsonage
           JOCELYN KELLETT AND DONALD HOPEWELL

     32    Haworth and its Parish Church
           IVY HOLGATE

     36    The Bronté Society
           EDITH WEIR

     42    The Bronté Society Transactions
           CHARLES LEMON

Coloured insert    A Tour of the Parsonage

# The story of the Brontës

*Sir Linton Andrews*

*Rev. Patrick Brontë.
1777–1861. Copied from an
original photograph (c. 1856)
by J. J. Stead*

Patrick Brunty, one of ten children, was born in a poor
little white-washed cottage in County Down on St.
Patrick's Day, 1777. No one would have expected him
to become the father of the most gifted family in our
literary history. He soon showed ambition and talent.
At the age of 16, after he had been a weaver, he was
already schoolmaster of a small village school. Then he
became tutor to the children of a Rector, who
encouraged him to aim at going to Cambridge. In due
course he enjoyed a sizarship at St. John's and became
a curate, first in Essex and then in Yorkshire, where he
was to spend the rest of his life. He published verse,
prose, pamphlets and sermons, none of them
foreshadowing the genius of two of his daughters,
Charlotte and Emily.

While he was at Wethersfield, in Essex, he sought to
marry a young woman, Mary Burder, who was well
off, but her uncle would not allow the marriage.
In 1812, when serving as a curate at Hartshead, near
Dewsbury, after being for a while at Dewsbury itself,
he married Maria Branwell, a Cornish woman, whom
he had met at Woodhouse Grove Wesleyan Academy
at Apperley Bridge, not far from Bradford. (By this
time Patrick was spelling his name Brontë, no doubt
because his hero, Lord Nelson, had been made Duke
of Brontë.) In one of her love letters Maria called Mr.
Brontë 'Dear saucy Pat'. He seems to have been genial

*The house in Market Street,
Thornton, where the four famous
Brontë children were born.*

and even flirtatious. There was still much of the peasant about him, but from being a barefoot urchin he had risen to a position of local importance.

Soon after setting up home at Hartshead, their first two children, Maria and Elizabeth, were born. Then, after an exchange of livings with the curate of Thornton, there were born Charlotte, Patrick Branwell, Emily Jane and Anne. It was in 1820, when all six children were under the age of 7, that the Brontës began their stay at Haworth that was to make that moorland township famous.

By this time Mrs. Brontë had become an invalid, and it was thought that the conditions at breezy Haworth would be healthier than at Thornton. Seven carts took the furniture, and probably the Brontës themselves, up the steep road to their new home. Mrs. Brontë then saw the grey stone Parsonage for the first time. She found the environment cold and bleak, and longed for her native Cornwall. Soon after her arrival she died of cancer. Her last words were, 'Oh, God, my poor children—oh, God, my poor children!'

During her illness her sister, Elizabeth, had come from Cornwall to nurse her, and now Aunt Branwell as she was always called, stayed on to look after the motherless family. The children had a lonely life in some respects, with more affection from the servant, Tabitha Aykroyd, than from their father, who said their prattle distressed him, reminding him of his dead wife. The only meal he had with them was breakfast. He then told blood-curdling tales of Ireland, Methodism and cotton riots. But he did encourage the children to think, and they were not harshly disciplined

The children relied very much on each other for their own happiness. In summer they found exceptional pleasure in wandering on the lonely moorland hills and among the tumbling becks. In winter they invented stories, probably in imitation of their father, or sat in the warm kitchen listening to Tabby. In 1824 all the children except Branwell and Anne were sent away to school. They must have felt it a cruel break to give up their happy life together. Maria and Elizabeth went in July, and Charlotte and Emily soon afterwards, to the newly-opened Clergy Daughters' School at Cowan Bridge, on the main road from Leeds to Kendal and about two miles from Kirkby Lonsdale. The founder was the Rev. William Carus Wilson, an evangelical of autocratic temperament. His idea was to provide an adequate education for the daughters of poor clergy at a small charge. But good intentions were not good enough to make it a good school. The discipline was harsh, and Maria suffered a great deal. She developed tuberculosis and presently was sent home to die at the age of eleven. Her father recorded that she exhibited during her illness many symptoms of a heart under divine influence.

Cooking conditions at the school were not as clean as they should have been, the building was an unhealthy one; low fever broke out and Elizabeth died. Mr. Brontë, alarmed, brought Charlotte and Emily home when Elizabeth fell ill, and there they stayed for some years.

Charlotte, when she was nine, found she must take Maria's place as mother to the other three. The school had made a horrifying impression on her mind. She was deeply embittered by Maria's death, and ever after thought of Cowan Bridge with dread. She was to describe it with savage loathing in *Jane Eyre*.

Now the children were at home all day their Aunt Branwell gave the three girls simple lessons, taught them sewing and home management, Methodist hymns and Methodist prayers full of hell-fire and eternal damnation. Mr. Brontë gave Greek and Latin lessons to Branwell. The girls, intensely shy, kept very much to themselves. Branwell, a popular boy, used to slip out to meet his friends.

We can now see the characters that developed so strongly later. Charlotte as the eldest took on responsibility. She liked managing and directing. She had ambition and wanted the others to be ambitious too. Emily had a proud, reserved and even stoical temperament. She was an independent, unconventional thinker. Anne, deeply religious, impressed all by her gentleness.

Playing together the children imagined adventures for their toy soldiers. The next step was to record these adventures. So began one of the most extraordinary literatures in existence, tiny books in microscopic writing which occupied the Brontës for years. More than a hundred of these little manuscript books exist, the smallest an inch and a half long. Some pages contain 1500 words. All the surviving books are by Charlotte and Branwell and deal with a mythical country named Angria. Emily and Anne had a rival saga devoted to the island of Gondal and a sister island. Altogether the children must have written millions of words. The stories are full of merciless fighting, unscrupulous assassinations, noble deaths, great struggles for power, loves and hates, triumphs and agonies. These were not just childish games. As Dr. Phyllis Bentley describes elsewhere in this book, they became almost a dominating fantasy in the lives of the Brontës. When they were grown up they found enormous pleasure in devising still more Gondal and Angrian adventures. They lived in two worlds—their shy, secluded, not unhappy life in the stone-floored Parsonage, and their life of escape and adventure and ambition in the heroic life of Angria and Gondal.

It was an astonishing apprenticeship to literature. The children might have some absurd ideas about social life, but they learned to use words with remarkable ease and variety. All the time they read eagerly. Meeting them you might have thought they were absurdly nervous and unattractive—even neurotic—but in some respects they were most precocious. André Gide speaks of a diary as the author's pocket mirror. The Brontës' childish writings did more than mirror their world. Thus Charlotte, a timid person with a fiery soul, was a slave to duty in ordinary life. Her heroines with infinite courage shape their own destinies.

When Charlotte was not yet fifteen she had again to face exile from home. She went as a boarder to Miss Margaret Wooler's school at Roe Head, not far from Dewsbury. Here, although unhappy and nervous at first, she made friends with Ellen Nussey and Mary and Martha Taylor. The new pupil was too short-sighted to play games but she worked hard in the schoolroom, and if politics were discussed she was acknowledged to be supreme. We know a great deal about her from her letters to Ellen Nussey, who was to remain her close friend and correspondent for the rest of her life. We

*Charlotte Brontë. 1816–1855. Pastel by George Richmond, RA. (National Portrait Gallery).*

know too that Mary and Martha Taylor were the originals of Rose and Jessy Yorke in *Shirley*. Charlotte was a pupil at Roe Head for about eighteen months, and when she returned, three years later, as a teacher there, she took Emily with her, but Emily, pining for home, was soon replaced by Anne.

Their outlook began to darken again. Branwell, who once did a translation of Horace which Coleridge praised, became not a famous author or artist but a booking-office clerk at Sowerby Bridge railway station; he took to drinking heavily and was dismissed. The girls tried being governesses but they hated it. You can imagine the family group at this time, each girl miserable when she was working as a governess, Emily, indeed, starting to waste away if robbed of her moorland solitudes. Charlotte was still set on making something of her brother and sisters. Emily pondered in mental solitude deep thoughts on life and death. Anne gave herself to doctrines like predestination. Branwell was always drinking, always borrowing money, bragging about what he could do, never doing it. He went to London to study at the Royal Academy, but apparently never attended there. He began to take opium.

A great turning point in the family's life came in 1842 when the sisters, with financial help from their aunt, thought of starting a school at the Parsonage. To acquire qualifications for teaching, Charlotte and Emily decided to go to Brussels to improve their foreign languages. They went to a school kept by Monsieur Constantin Heger and his wife. What an extraordinary pair they must have seemed in that school. They were dowdy, unsociable and as shy as

*Part of a letter from Charlotte Brontë to William Smith Williams, dated January 22, 1848. It refers to the confusion of identity by the use of pseudonyms. (4 pp. Size 7¾ × 4½ ins. Bonnell Collection, 196).*

ever, but they were determined to learn, and learn they did. Miss Branwell's death brought them back, but Charlotte returned to the school at Brussels. There, very miserable, she longed for home. Her only comfort was the encouragement M. Heger gave her. She fell deeply in love with him. I do not think her abject devotion to the man, a most stimulating teacher, can be described in any other way. It is hard to think that he responded sentimentally to her obvious affection for him. He may occasionally have paid her compliments out of kindness.

A correspondence between them after she returned home for good had a remarkable end. M. Heger suggested that Charlotte in future should address her letters to him not at the school where he lived but at

Patrick Branwell Brontë

another where he did some teaching. This no doubt was in order to keep the correspondence secret from his wife. Charlotte thought the suggestion intolerable. She felt bleak disillusionment, and never wrote to M. Heger again.

She was plunged into deeper depression than ever. Branwell, whom she despised for his weakness, brought more shame and humiliation upon the family by his infatuation for his employer's wife. He was summarily dismissed by the Rev. Edmund Robinson, to whose son he was tutor and to whose daughters Anne was governess. Mr. Robinson died not long afterwards. Branwell hoped to marry the wealthy widow, but she wanted to have nothing more to do with the young man. Branwell's hopes seem to have been fantastic. Drinking heavily and making everybody in the house wretched, he sank into hopeless ruin. His disappointment may be said to have killed him.

Think of the gloom at the Parsonage. Charlotte had had the most crushing humiliation of her life. Branwell was both spiritually and physically ruined. Emily, always kind to the helpless, felt towards the wretched Branwell the sympathy that Charlotte could not show, but must have felt heart-broken. Poor, gentle Anne must have needed all the consolation that religion afforded.

The proposal for a school had come to nothing. Prospectuses had been sent out, but no parents wanted to send their children to Haworth. Now that Branwell, a drunkard, an opium taker and an almost insane nuisance, lived at home there was no chance of establishing a school at the Parsonage. What an outlook! Whence could the harassed sisters look for rescue?

One of the extraordinary things about the Brontës is that in all their early plans for earning a living they did not try to write novels for publication much earlier. People who write usually have a craving to get into print. The sisters' first published works appeared in 1846, when Charlotte was 30, but this was a venture for fame rather than fortune. They had put together a little volume of verses, using as their pseudonyms Currer Bell for Charlotte, Ellis Bell for Emily, and Acton Bell for Anne. The initials corresponded but some motive of delicacy or discretion prevented the sisters from assuming a clearly different sex.

Some of the poems, Emily's, were remarkably strong and original, though with technical blemishes, but only two copies of the book were sold. Then Charlotte wrote a novel, *The Professor*, based on her life at Brussels and a master-pupil theme, but though it was a tender love story with a delightful heroine no publisher would accept the book. The three-volume novel then prevailed and *The Professor* would have made only two volumes. But the publishers, Smith and Elder, gave the author encouragement and she produced a work of the right length, *Jane Eyre*. The right length was the least of its attractions, and the book scored an almost instantaneous success. Its fiery passion and sensitive writing took the public by storm. It was entirely new for a novelist to portray a woman declaring her love for a man and claiming the right to feel and express passion.

Emily's *Wuthering Heights* appeared soon after *Jane Eyre*.

This was a shortish novel, but Anne's story, *Agnes Grey*, helped to fill out the necessary three volumes. *Wuthering Heights*, for all its wonderful quality, made little impression at first on the reading public and it was not till long after Emily's death that it became widely acknowledged as a work of genius.

The publishers did not know that Currer, Ellis and Acton Bell were women until Charlotte went to see them in London with Anne, whose second novel, *The Tenant of Wildfell Hall*, had now been published. The sisters then revealed their identity in one of the oddest scenes in literary history.

Sorrow still haunted the Parsonage. Branwell died in September 1848 at the age of 31. Emily, stoically rejecting sympathy during her sufferings, died at the age of 30 the following December, not knowing that she was destined to be famous, and Anne, 29, died at Scarborough in May the next year. Charlotte and her old father were left together at the Parsonage. Although she came to know people like Thackeray, Mrs. Gaskell and Harriet Martineau, Charlotte never reached terms of close friendship with them. She was melancholy, neurotic and distressingly self-conscious, yet on paper she laid bare the innermost secrets of a woman's passion.

*Shirley* was written at a time of the deepest gloom— Emily died shortly after it was begun and Anne before it was finished—yet it had many bright pages. Then followed *Villette*, in which Charlotte returned to her master-pupil theme. But though she was still dominated by the memory of Constantin Heger, she at last consented to marry her father's curate, Arthur

Bell Nicholls, who had long admired her. She had ridiculed him to her friend Ellen Nussey. She must have thought him intensely narrow-minded, but there was something in his strong, rugged nature that she came to like. Her father at first angrily resisted the match, but at last he yielded.

Charlotte as a wife was happier than she expected; she enjoyed being cared for. But within a year she died at the age of 38, of a complication of pregnancy, continual nausea and probably tuberculosis. Her small body was worn out. On her death bed she murmured, 'Oh, I am not going to die, am I? He will not separate us. We have been so happy.'

Mrs. Gaskell wrote a classic biography of Charlotte. It was a sad story, but Mary Taylor said it was not so gloomy as the truth and that Charlotte Brontë had lived all her days in a walking nightmare of poverty and self-suppression. Self-suppression? No. She had expressed herself more openly on paper than any other writer in English literature. There is no family quite like the Brontës in literary history. There are few life stories so full of sadness.

Poor Charlotte! She tried so hard to make something of herself, something of her sisters and brother. Though often frustrated in her ambitions she did succeed as a writer and knew herself famous. Emily was not so fortunate in her lifetime. Her genius was slow to gain recognition, but now she is acclaimed no less than Charlotte and her strange, stoical mind is now the subject of much fascinated study. The two sisters have an immortal place in our literature.

Their father lived on in the old house as incumbent until his death in 1861 at the age of 84. Charlotte's husband, who went back to Ireland after Mr. Brontë's death, married again and died in 1906 when almost 90.

# Chronology

*Juliet R. V. Barker*

| | | |
|---|---|---|
| 1777 | March 17 | Patrick Brontë born at Emdale, County Down, Ireland. |
| 1783 | April 15 | Maria Branwell born at Penzance, Cornwall. |
| 1802 | | Patrick Brontë entered St. John's College, Cambridge. |
| 1806 | | Curate at Wethersfield. |
| 1809 | | Curate at Wellington, Salop. |
| 1809 | | Curate at Dewsbury, Yorkshire. |
| 1811 | | Curate at Hartshead-cum-Clifton, Yorkshire. |
| 1812 | | Maria Branwell visited her uncle, John Fennell, at Woodhouse Grove School, Apperley Bridge. |
| 1812 | December 29 | Marriage of Patrick Brontë and Maria Branwell at Guiseley Church. |
| 1814 | | Maria Brontë born; baptised April 23, at Hartshead. |
| 1815 | February 8 | Elizabeth Brontë born; baptised August 26, at Thornton. |
| 1815 | | Mr. Brontë incumbent of Thornton, Bradford. |
| 1816 | April 21 | Charlotte Brontë born; baptised at Thornton, June 29. |
| 1817 | June 26 | Patrick Branwell born; baptised at Thornton, July 23. |
| 1818 | July 30 | Emily Jane born; baptised at Thornton, August 20. |
| 1820 | January 17 | Anne born; baptised at Thornton, March 25. |
| 1820 | February | Mr. Brontë incumbent of Haworth. |
| 1821 | September 15 | Mrs. Brontë died and was buried at Haworth Church. Her eldest sister, Miss Elizabeth Branwell, took charge of the family. |
| 1824 | July | Maria and Elizabeth went to Cowan Bridge School. |
| 1824 | August | Charlotte went to Cowan Bridge School. |
| 1824 | November | Emily went to Cowan Bridge School. |
| 1825 | February 14 | Maria left in ill health, died May 6. |
| 1825 | May 31 | Elizabeth left in ill health, died June 15. |
| 1825 | June 1 | Charlotte and Emily left the school. |
| 1825 | | Tabitha Aykroyd came as servant to the Parsonage, and stayed for over thirty years. |
| 1831 | January | Charlotte went to Miss Wooler's school at Roe Head, and there met her life long friends, Ellen Nussey and Mary Taylor. |
| 1832 | July | Charlotte left Roe Head to teach her sisters at home. |
| 1835 | July | Charlotte returned to Roe Head as a teacher, accompanied by Emily as a pupil. Emily stayed only two months, then Anne took her place, staying till December 1837. |

| | | |
|---|---|---|
| 1835 | | Branwell went to London to study at the Royal Academy but returned, for unknown reasons, within a few days. |
| 1838 | June | Branwell set up as a portrait painter in Bradford, lodging with Mrs. Kirby at 3, Fountain Street. Returned home in debt May 1839. |
| 1838 | September | Emily went as a teacher to Miss Patchett's school at Law Hill, Southowram, Halifax, but only stayed for six months. |
| 1838 | December | Charlotte finally left her teaching post at Roe Head. |
| 1839 | April | Anne went as a governess to Mrs. Ingham, Blake Hall, Mirfield, and left December 1839. |
| 1839 | May | Charlotte went as a governess to Mrs. Sidgwick, Stonegappe Hall, Lothersdale, and left July 1839. |
| 1839 | August | Rev. William Weightman appointed curate of Haworth. |
| 1839 | September | Charlotte and Ellen Nussey visited Bridlington, staying with Mr. and Mrs. Hudson at Easton. |
| 1840 | January-June | Branwell went as a tutor to Mr. Postlethwaite's sons at Broughton-in-Furness. |
| 1840 | May | Anne went as a governess to Mrs. Robinson, Thorp Green Hall, Little Ouseburn, near York. |
| 1840 | September | Branwell became a clerk on the new railway at Sowerby Bridge. |
| 1841 | March | Charlotte went as a governess to Mrs. White, Upperwood House, Rawdon. |
| 1841 | April | Branwell promoted to Clerk-in-Charge and transferred to Luddenden Foot. |
| 1841 | December | Charlotte left Upperwood House. |
| 1842 | February | Charlotte and Emily went to Brussels to study at the Pensionnat Heger. |
| 1842 | April | Branwell dismissed from Luddenden Foot. |
| 1842 | September 6 | Death of William Weightman. |
| 1842 | October 29 | Death of Miss Elizabeth Branwell. |
| 1842 | November | Charlotte and Emily return to Haworth. |
| 1843 | January | Charlotte returned to Brussels, leaving Emily to keep house for her father; Branwell went back with Anne to Thorp Green as tutor to Edmund Robinson. |
| 1844 | January | Charlotte finally left Brussels and returned to Haworth. |
| 1844 | August | Rev. Arthur Bell Nicholls appointed curate of Haworth. |
| 1845 | June | Anne left Thorp Green. |
| 1845 | July | Branwell dismissed from Thorp Green. |
| 1845 | July | Charlotte stayed with Ellen Nussey at Hathersage, Derbyshire. |
| 1846 | May | Publication of *Poems* by Currer, Ellis and Acton Bell. *The Professor* written by Charlotte and refused by various publishers. *Agnes Grey* written by Anne, and *Wuthering Heights* written by Emily about this time. |

| 1846 August | Charlotte took her father to Manchester for a cataract operation, and commenced her novel *Jane Eyre*. |
| 1847 October | *Jane Eyre* published. |
| 1847 December | *Wuthering Heights* and *Agnes Grey* published. |
| 1848 July | Charlotte and Anne visited the publisher, Mr. George Smith, in London, to establish their identity because of a misunderstanding with an American firm of publishers. |
| 1848 July | *The Tenant of Wildfell Hall* published. |
| 1848 September 24 | Branwell died, aged 31. |
| 1848 December 19 | Emily Jane died, aged 30. |
| 1849 May 28 | Anne died, aged 29, at Scarborough, and was buried in St. Mary's churchyard. |
| 1849 June | Charlotte stayed for a second time with Mrs. Hudson, at Easton Farm, Bridlington, and continued her third novel *Shirley*. |
| 1849 October | Publication of *Shirley*. |
| 1849 December | Charlotte stayed with Mr. George Smith and his mother in London, and met Thackeray and Harriet Martineau. |
| 1850 March | Charlotte visited Sir James Kay-Shuttleworth at Gawthorpe Hall, Lancashire. |
| 1850 June | Stayed again with Mr. George Smith and his family in London, met G. H. Lewes and Miss Kavanagh, attended dinner party at Thackeray's home in Young Street, and sat for her portrait to George Richmond. (This portrait is now in the National Portrait Gallery.) |
| 1850 July | Charlotte visited Edinburgh with Mr. George Smith. |
| 1850 August | Charlotte stayed with Sir James Kay-Shuttleworth at Briery Close, Windermere, and made the acquaintance of Mrs. Gaskell. |
| 1850 December | Charlotte visited Harriet Martineau at The Knoll, Windermere. About this time she started writing *Villette*. |
| 1851 May-June | Charlotte visited London for The Great Exhibition and attended the Thackeray lectures. |
| 1851 June | Charlotte stayed with Mrs. Gaskell at Plymouth Grove. |
| 1852 June | Charlotte stayed alone at Filey, and visited Anne's grave at Scarborough. |
| 1852 December | Publication of her fourth and last novel *Villette*. |
| 1852 December | Rev. A. B. Nicholls proposed marriage to Charlotte. Her father violently objected, and Mr. Nicholls later resigned his curacy at Haworth and went to Kirksmeaton, May 1853. |
| 1853 January | Charlotte's last visit to London. |
| 1853 April | Charlotte spent a week with Mrs. Gaskell in Manchester. In September of that year Mrs. Gaskell came to visit her at Haworth. |
| 1853 September | Charlotte stayed with Miss Wooler at Hornsea. |
| 1854 January | Mr. Nicholls stayed with his friend, Mr. Grant, near Haworth, and Mr. Brontë gradually withdrew his objections to the marriage. The engagement was formally announced April 1854. |

| | | |
|---|---|---|
| 1854 May | | Mr. Nicholls resumed his duties as curate of Haworth. |
| 1854 June 29 | | Charlotte and Mr. Nicholls were married at Haworth Church by the Rev. Sutcliffe Sowden. Miss Wooler gave her away, and Ellen Nussey acted as bridesmaid. They went to Conway and Bangor for their honeymoon, then crossed to Ireland, visiting Dublin, Cork, Killarney, and Mr. Nicholls' old home at Banagher. Here they met Mr. Nicholls' cousin, Miss Mary Bell, who was later to become the second Mrs. Nicholls. |
| 1855 January | | Charlotte and her husband visited Sir James Kay-Shuttleworth at Gawthorpe Hall. Charlotte caught a chill walking on wet grass, from which she never recovered. |
| 1855 February | | Tabitha Aykroyd, the beloved servant of the Brontë family, died, aged 84. |
| 1855 March 31 | | Death of Charlotte, aged 38. |
| 1855 June | | Mr. Brontë wrote to Mrs. Gaskell, suggesting she should write a brief life of Charlotte Brontë. |
| 1857 | | Publication of Mrs. Gaskell's *Life of Charlotte Brontë.* |
| 1857 | | Publication of Charlotte's first novel *The Professor* with a preface by Mr. Nicholls. |
| 1861 June 7 | | Rev. Patrick Brontë died, aged 84. Mr. Nicholls left Haworth, and returned to live in his native Ireland. |
| 1878 | | Gabled wing added to Parsonage by the Rev. John Wade, successor to Patrick Brontë. |
| 1879 | | Haworth Church demolished, and replaced by present building. |
| 1893 December 16 | | The Brontë Society founded at a meeting at Bradford Town Hall, with Lord Houghton as first President. |
| 1895 May 18 | | The Brontë Museum opened in the upper floor of The Yorkshire Penny Bank, at Haworth. |
| 1897 November 26 | | Death of Ellen Nussey, aged 80. |
| 1906 | | Mr. Nicholls died at his home at Banagher, Ireland. |
| 1928 | | Haworth Parsonage bought by Sir James Roberts, a native of Haworth, and given to The Brontë Society as a Brontë Museum. |
| 1929 | | Bonnell collection of Brontë manuscripts, letters and books donated to the Brontë Society. |
| 1944 | | Brontë memorial tablet placed in Poet's Corner, Westminster Abbey. |
| 1947 | | Formal handing over of memorial tablet. |
| 1960 | | Bonnell Room and Extension to Parsonage opened. |
| 1964 July 4 | | Brontë Memorial Chapel in Haworth Church dedicated. |
| 1975 | | Seton Gordon Manuscript Collection donated to the Brontë Society. |
| 1980 | | Important Brontë manuscripts from the Grolier Collection bought by the Brontë Society. |
| 1985 | | Brontë portraits return to Brontë Parsonage Museum for first time in National Portrait Gallery touring exhibition. |

# The novels of the Brontës

*Phyllis Bentley*

It must always be remembered that the Rev. Patrick Brontë was himself in early life a man of literary ambition. Two volumes of poems (*Cottage Poems* and *The Rural Minstrel*) and two prose fictions (*The Cottage in the Wood* and *The Maid of Killarney*, or *Albion and Flora*) were published from his pen in 1811 and 1813, the last-named in London, the others by booksellers in Yorkshire towns. By the standards of today, Mr. Brontë's verses are poor and his tales tedious, but all the same they play a significant part in his children's lives. For the children were from their earliest days accustomed to the sight of printed books bearing the name of Brontë on their title-page, and the idea of writing for publication was thus familiar and desirable to them. 'We had very early cherished the dream of one day becoming authors', wrote Charlotte after she had achieved fame.

How their genius first began to express itself in the writing of fiction is a fascinating story. On the night of June 5, 1826—that is, when Charlotte was ten, and Branwell, Emily and Anne slightly younger—Mr. Brontë brought home from Leeds a box of twelve wooden soldiers for Branwell. Next morning Branwell gleefully showed the soldiers to his sisters, and allowed each to choose one of the soldiers and become its patron. Charlotte chose the handsomest and named him after her great hero, the Duke of Wellington. The children began to 'make-believe' about these Young Men, or the Twelves, as they called them, inventing and telling each other stories of their adventures. Stimulated by the section on Africa in Goldsmith's *A Grammar of General Geography*—their copy is in the Bonnell room for you to see—they sent the Twelves to the West African coast, where they founded a group of kingdoms called the Great Glasstown Confederacy, under the rule of the wooden Duke of Wellington, each soldier having a kingdom of his own. By 1829 the young Brontës were writing the Twelves' adventures, in minute handwriting, in tiny homemade books, often only two-and-a-half inches by one-and-a-half in size.

The daydream kingdom of Glasstown gradually grew into a whole world, containing everything a real world could show: poets, prime ministers; parliaments, public-houses; generals, armies; magazines, picture galleries, love-affairs; all most romantically treated. A son of the imaginary Wellington, the Duke of Zamorna, conquered another kingdom and became King of Angria. Meanwhile Emily and Anne decided to leave Glasstown, and found a kingdom of their own: Gondal, an imaginary island in the Pacific, ruled over by an imperious queen. No prose Gondal work written by Emily or Anne is now in existence, as far as we know, though the titles of some are mentioned by the girls in their birthday notes; many of Emily's

*Branwell's manuscript newspaper,*
The Monthly Intelligencer, *and two of the miniature books written by the Brontë children. The writing desk belonged to Anne.*

poems also were written about Gondal. Of Charlotte's and Branwell's Angrian writings, however, enough remain to equal in length the whole of the Brontës' published works.

The Brontës continued writing about their imaginary worlds (on larger pages as they grew older, but in the same small hand-writing) long after they ceased to be children: indeed it is probable that Emily never gave up her daydreams. But with Charlotte there came a time when she felt she must have a change from the Angrian scene. 'I long,' she wrote, 'to quit for awhile that burning clime where we have sojourned too long— the mind would cease from excitement and turn now to a cooler region where the dawn breaks grey and sober'.

Thus when Charlotte began to write her first novel of the real world, *The Professor*, she was determined that it should be plain and homely. But in fact the first six chapters of *The Professor*, during which the hero, William Crimsworth, works in the West Riding mill of his purse-proud brother, are still tinged with Angrian melodrama. It is only when Crimsworth reaches Brussels and begins to teach in a boys' school there under the worldly M. Pelet and in the girls' school next door under the equally detestable directress, Mlle. Zoräide Reuter, that realism begins. This part of the book is drawn, of course, from Charlotte's own experience in Brussels at the Heger school, only that she has reversed the nationalities of herself and her admired M. Heger in the pair of lovers, making the schoolmaster an Englishman, and the young pupil-teacher, Frances Henri, whom he loves, as Charlotte wished M. Heger would have loved her, partly French.

The realism of Charlotte's account of the two schools, and particularly of the girls whom Crimsworth teaches, is exceedingly bitter. It is hardly surprising that *The Professor* was refused by publishers nine times, and not published until 1857, two years after Charlotte's death. Yet Charlotte is right when she says that *The Professor* has force and pith, and that it gives a new view of a certain type of character; she was the first English novelist to treat of school-teachers and the schoolroom as on the same level of interest and passion as princes and palaces.

*Jane Eyre* (published in 1847) has always been the popular favourite among Charlotte Brontë's novels, and this is not to be wondered at, for it tells a superbly exciting story about characters so strongly and vividly drawn that they have become household words. The orphaned Jane, poor, plain and friendless, excites the reader's warmest sympathy throughout. Bullied at her rich aunt's, wretched at Lowood school, venturing into the great world as governess to Edward Rochester's illegitimate child, bravely extinguishing the fire lighted by Rochester's mad wife, despairing at her frustrated wedding, rejecting Rochester's dishonourable proposals, stumbling homeless through the night — throughout these harrowing trials Jane is always a soul made of fire; a free human being with an independent will, as she proudly says; a woman compact of passion and integrity. The interlude with St. John Rivers and his sisters is less interesting, a trifle flat indeed after the tremendous drama of Thornfield Hall; but this is a legitimate presentment of life as it appears to those crossed in love. Jane's story presents in exciting form the perennial problem of the woman on her own, with her living to earn and no advantages, who has yet the right and the power to love. The problem is as pressing today as it was in Charlotte's time, and this contemporary relevance is probably one of the factors in Jane's persistent popularity.

In *Jane Eyre* Charlotte has achieved a perfect fusion of realism and romance. The romantic figure of Rochester, masterful, immoral, fascinating, might have been mere luridly painted cardboard, but that uncomfortable little flibbertigibbet of a daughter, Adèle, drawn with such uncompromising truth as the heir of her mother's lightness; the honest Mrs. Fairfax with her conventional limitations; the fact that Rochester is blinded and disgraced, no fairy prince, when Jane at length marries him; the detailed miseries of Lowood — all these paint in the shadows which give the romantic situation three dimensions.

In *Shirley* (1849) we are in a different world. 'If you think that anything like a romance is preparing for you, reader,' wrote Charlotte on the first page, 'you never were more mistaken. Calm your expectations; something real, cool and solid lies before you; something unromantic as Monday morning.' *Shirley* is indeed a daylight novel, set in a wide industrial landscape, teeming with external action.

The setting is the West Riding of Yorkshire in 1812, when machinery was introduced into the textile mills by the manufacturers and attacked by their workers who feared unemployment. In 1812 Mr. Brontë had resided near Rawfolds Mills, the scene of one of the most violent attacks by the unhappy Luddites, as the conspiring workers called themselves. From his reminiscences, and a careful study of contemporary newspaper reports, Charlotte fashioned her plot. In this no less than four household groups of characters play their part: the sweet Caroline Helstone and her unsympathetic uncle, the vicar; Shirley Keeldar the heiress, said to be drawn from Emily Brontë, intelligent, impetuous, 'sister of the spotted, bright, quick, fiery leopard', with her diffident chaperon, Mrs. Pryor, and her great dog Tartar; Robert Moore the half-Yorkshire half-Belgian manufacturer whom Caroline loves, with his eccentric sister Hortense; Hiram Yorke, that intensely Yorkshire millowner, and his turbulent family, drawn from Charlotte's Taylor friends.

Robust and vigorous in its earlier pages, the novel loses some of its force after the tragic deaths of Charlotte's sisters struck her such terrible blows, and the division of interest between the two heroines, Caroline and Shirley, impairs its artistic unity. But the minor characters, richly varied, are superbly drawn, and as one of the earliest regional novels and industrial novels in English literature, *Shirley* is strikingly original.

In *Villette* (1853) we return to the confined scene and the intense inner conflict. Like *The Professor*, *Villette* is based on Charlotte's experiences in Brussels, but this second version is far finer than the first. For here Charlotte has dared to tell the story of the Brussels school and the love of master and pupil from her own point of view; Lucy Snowe, who becomes a teacher in Madame Beck's girls' school and loves M. Paul Emanuel, has all Charlotte's terrible force of feeling and passionate integrity, hidden beneath the demure and cool exterior which Charlotte as well as Lucy took

pains to preserve. The result is a masterpiece whenever Lucy, Madame Beck and M. Paul are on the scene. The minor characters are not completely convincing, though Dr. Bretton has the makings of a subtle study if Charlotte's plan—or perhaps her courage, for he is said to have been drawn from her publisher, George Smith—had permitted her to develop him more fully.

An unfinished fragment of a novel entitled *Emma* leaves us regretting more than ever Charlotte's early death, for it shows all her accustomed force and poignancy in a different turn of story. Emma's father drives up to a small boarding-school and deposits her with a wealthy flourish, then disappears. The fees are left unpaid, the address he gave proves false. The vulgar headmistress attacks the child, whose silent agony shows her unwilling knowledge of her father's deception. Here the fragment ends. This new rendering of Charlotte's favourite theme, integrity against the world, promised a fascinating story.

*Wuthering Heights* (1847), Emily Brontë's single but superb novel, received little appreciation in her lifetime, but now is recognised as a masterpiece unique in English fiction. No English novelist has impressed a fiction setting on the reader's mind more vividly and memorably, with more majestic beauty, than Emily. The West Riding moors with their wild weather— 'the power of the north wind blowing over the edge'— enter the book in its very title, for *wuthering*, as Emily tells us, is a significant provincial adjective descriptive of the atmospheric tumult to which the house is exposed in stormy weather. The wild and sombre moorland landscape continues to be present on every page, recorded from most penetrating observation in powerful and poetic phrases, until the last exquisite scene where the graves of Catherine, Edgar Linton and Heathcliff lie quietly under a benign evening sky amid the heath and the harebells. Emily's prose style resembles her beloved moors. Her writing is plain and bare, with no fanciful turns, no glittering images, no unnecessary adjectives, but strong and bold in outline as the rocks and deep in tone as the purple heather.

The plot of *Wuthering Heights*, far from being the confused and sprawling affair which some readers have supposed, is a neat and powerful network of cause and effect, shapely in its symmetry, mighty in the strength of its motivation. It presents the effect on two families of a disordering cause, rashly introduced, which jars all the evil in their natures into action. Up on the edge of the moors at Wuthering Heights live the four Earnshaws, fiercely independent farming stock; down in the valley at Thrushcross Grange live the four Lintons, mildly genteel. Mr. Earnshaw brings home from Liverpool the strange child Heathcliff. Love, jealousy, scorn, hate, revenge, spring into being at Heathcliff's touch, ever increasing as yet another person of the group receives the fatal impact; they spread to the next generation; at last the action, coming full circle, pierces Heathcliff's own breast.

Though the plot is thus bold and simple, the structure of the narrative seems complicated. The story is told to us partly by Mr. Lockwood, a stranger to the neighbourhood, and partly by the housekeeper Nelly Dean, and Nelly often tells us what other people told her. (But this is surely how we learn stories in real life.) The novel begins near the end of the story, when Mr. Lockwood visits Wuthering Heights and finds

Heathcliff, Cathy and Hareton there, involved in a mysterious relationship of hate. Gradually the origins and course of this relationship are revealed to us, the past by Nelly, the present chiefly by Mr. Lockwood. The elemental human passions of this stormy tale are portrayed by Emily with unrelenting force, but also with impartial compassion. She sees the fearful results which follow because Catherine is selfish, Edgar weak, Heathcliff savage, Isabella peevish, Cathy wilful, but she does not condemn the human beings whose fate drives them to display these qualities.

It has sometimes been said that Branwell Brontë was the author of part or all of *Wuthering Heights*. Anyone who reads Branwell's pompous and arid prose in his childhood writings will doubt this, and the evidence on which the theory rested has been shown to be very dubious—it was almost certainly Branwell's own tedious and over-written fragment, *And the Weary Are at Rest*, which, read to his friends, was mistaken by them later for a chapter of *Wuthering Heights*. It is worth noticing that the only character whom Emily portrays harshly in her novel is Hindley Earnshaw who, like Branwell, is a drunkard.

Anne Brontë's writing lacks the force and colour of her sisters', but it has a quiet dignity and precision of its own. The heroine of her novel *Agnes Grey* (1847) is another of the little governesses whose adventures, so restricted yet so deeply felt, are depicted by the Brontës with such keen sympathy, such authentic detail. Like Anne, Agnes suffers first in the house of purse-proud manufacturers, then in the mansion of fashionable county gentry. She loves the curate, as

Anne probably loved her father's curate, William Weightman, is separated from him as Anne was, but unlike poor Anne, finds happiness with him in the end. *Agnes Grey* has been compared by George Moore to a dress of white muslin, exquisitely cut. A comparison more in tune with Anne's determined anti-romanticism is that of a milk pudding, innocuous in appearance but containing an unexpectedly strong dose of nutmeg; for the novel's mild and pious plan is strongly flavoured by keenly sardonic observations on fond parents, naughty children, eloquent vicars, coarse uncles, even an unpleasing grandmama.

Charlotte considered the subject of Anne's other novel, *The Tenant of Wildfell Hall* (1848), an entire mistake, but the modern reader will not altogether agree. The character of Arthur Huntingdon is drawn from the unfortunate Branwell, and reveals the drunkard, not in the exhilaration of an orgy, but as his family sees him from day to day, in the sick peevishness of gradual deterioration. Anne thought it her duty to present this character as a warning, and her meticulous observation and precise rendering of detail make it a warning indeed. The other characters, insolent in their intrigues and quarrels, may or may not have been seen by Anne in the house of her aristocratic employers, the Robinsons, but are uncertainly drawn and do not greatly engage the reader's interest. The structure of the book is interesting: it falls into three parts, each narrated by the person who suffers most during its course.

If the Brontës' novels are subjected to a critical enquiry as to the kind and degree of impression which they make upon the reader, they emerge as unique in kind and of a very high intensity. Their stories, characters, settings and point of view are entirely original, while the strange pungent blend of Celtic poetry and sardonic Yorkshire realism in which they are presented is not to be found in any other novel. A fierce personal integrity stamps all their work. The depth of impression they make upon readers may be measured by their continuing popularity after a century. Plays, books, films, radio and television programmes about the Brontës and their lives, appear in abundance today and are always well received; the number of visitors to Haworth steadily rises. The Brontë's place in English literature is assured.

*Anne Brontë, a pencil drawing by Charlotte authenticated by Mr. Brontë.*

# The Brontës as poets

*Wilfred Rowland Childe*

The poetry of the Brontës is an expression with two meanings, as we are now accustomed to use the word poetry in two senses, the one referring to form, the other to content. The Brontë novels are suffused with poetry in the second sense, and Charlotte, who when she writes poetry in verse is on the whole moralistic and tedious, has filled *Jane Eyre*, to take one example, with the very spirit of poetry. But the gift of poetry came to her only when she wrote prose. When she attempts verse, she projects into the lines only her every-day self, the intensely moral, rather narrow personality which shows itself in many of her letters. In Charlotte's case the dichotomy of soul is very marked. Her genius taught her the place of passion in life, but in actual life she was repressed and almost respectable.

There was in Emily a fusion of passion and imagination which makes her an essentially greater figure and accounts for the extraordinary character of her poetry, both in verse and prose. Whereas Charlotte's prose is frequently poetic, her verse is almost entirely prosaic and lacks the deeper poetic sensibilities. You cannot say it is, generally speaking, bad, though all the Brontës, even including Emily, had tendencies towards melodrama, but whatever it is, it is not very good poetry. Take this stanza, for instance, which is well above the average of her verse:

> But there are hours of lonely musing,
>     Such as in evening silence come,
> When, soft as birds their pinions closing,
>     The heart's best feelings gather home.

> Then in our souls there seems to languish,
>     A tender grief that is not woe
> And thoughts that once wrung groans of anguish,
>     Now cause but some mild tears to flow.

The whole effect is curiously tepid from the artistic point of view, though it seems to possess Charlotte's usual sincerity and moral integrity. But these qualities will not necessarily produce good poetry, which requires a certain degree of ecstasy. Emily's 'God of Visions' did not visit Charlotte when she wrote verse, though his presence is discernible in Lucy Snowe wandering through the streets of Brussels or Jane Eyre tormented by thirst on the moor.

In Charlotte's finest poem, *Retrospect*, there is an extraordinary freshness and immediacy, a personal note quite lacking in the rest of her verse, which shows the continual presence of a poetic convention:

> We wove a web in childhood,
>     A web of sunny air;
> We dug a spring in infancy
>     Of water pure and fair;

*We sowed in youth a mustard seed,*
 *We cut an almond rod :*
*We are now grown up to a riper age ;*
 *Are they withered in the sod ?*

*Are they blighted, failed and faded ?*
 *Are they mouldered back to clay ?*
*For life is darkly shaded*
 *And its joys fleet fast away.*

There is something thrilling in hearing for once an authentic voice. It is as though the veils of conventional album-poetry were swept aside and a small but real poetic talent were revealed.

The poetry of Anne, though not of the first rank, is much better than Charlotte's because it expresses a more direct and immediate feeling, a quality of simplicity and humility. There is a strong note of genuine pathos. Anne wrote poetry as a bird sings, but Charlotte like somebody repeating a lesson. There is something almost Wordsworthian (a note found fairly often in Emily's poems too) in the bareness and purity of Anne at her best. Consider this, for instance :

*For ever hang thy dreamy spell*
*Round mountain star and heather bell,*
 *And do not pass away*
*From sparkling frost or wreathed snow,*
*And whisper when the wild winds blow*
 *Or rippling waters play.*

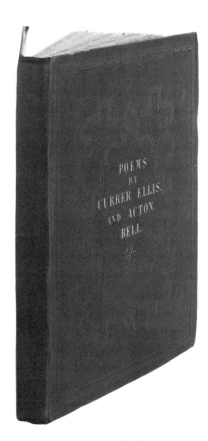

*First issue of* **Poems**, *with cloth binding bearing 'geometrical rules' design and front lettering, published by Aylott and Jones in 1846.*

# A tour of the Parsonage

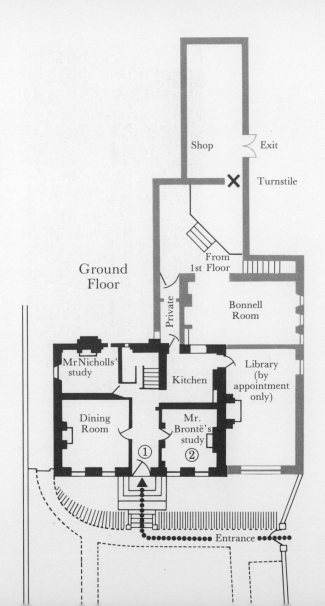

Shop　Exit

Turnstile

From
1st Floor

Ground
Floor

Private

Bonnell
Room

Mr Nicholls'
study

Kitchen

Library
(by
appointment
only)

Dining
Room

Mr.
Brontë's
study

① ②

Entrance

## 1. Entrance

This Georgian house was built in 1778 of local stone. A century later, the Rev. John Wade, who took Mr. Brontë's place as incumbent, added the gable wing. This now houses the library and exhibition room. The original Brontë part of the house contains the Brontë furniture and the family's personal belongings. The building was presented to the Brontë Society in 1928 by Sir James Roberts, a native of Haworth. Charlotte carried out various alterations to the house, enlarging the dining room and bedroom above, at the expense of the hall and nursery. Most of the furniture belonged to the Brontës and the decorations are of the period.

## 2. Mr. Brontë's Study

The room on the right was Mr. Brontë's study where he worked, and interviewed his parishioners. It contains Emily's piano, drawings by Charlotte of Anne's dog Flossy and a large engraving of John Martin's *Last Judgement*. On the table, Mr. Brontë's tobacco jar, pipe and spectacles lie by his Book of Psalms. His stout walking sticks, and stovepipe hat are ready to hand.

### 3. The Dining Room

This room is the one in which the sisters did much of their work. It contains the rocking chair where Anne used to sit with her feet on the fender and the sofa on which Emily died. Mrs. Gaskell, Charlotte's biographer, wrote that the prevailing colour of the room was crimson..Charlotte wrote: 'We have got curtains for the dining room. I ordered them at the factory to be dyed crimson, but they are badly dyed and do not please me.' Over the mantel-piece hangs a copy of Richmond's portrait of Charlotte; over the sofa is Leyland's plaster medallion portrait of Patrick Branwell Brontë. On the other wall there are engravings of two of Charlotte's heroes, the Duke of Wellington and William Makepeace Thackeray. The room was enlarged by Charlotte when she became a successful writer.

### 4. Mr. Nicholls' Study

This room was converted from a store room entered only from the yard. In May 1854 Charlotte altered the floor levels, built a fire place and put in a new window in order to make a study for her husband-to-be. On the walls are pew doors from Haworth Old Church which was demolished in 1879.

### 5. The Kitchen

The room became a passage in the 1878 alterations and the Society has endeavoured to reconstruct a kitchen of the type that was in use in the time of the Brontës. It was here that Tabitha spent much of her time talking to the children. Originally there was also a back kitchen where much of the work would be done but this vanished in the alterations. The fire-range is not original but of the period. The furnishings and exhibits have returned to their original home; many of them were purchased at the sale of Brontë effects in 1861, including a copper and brass tea-urn bought then for 17/- (85p).

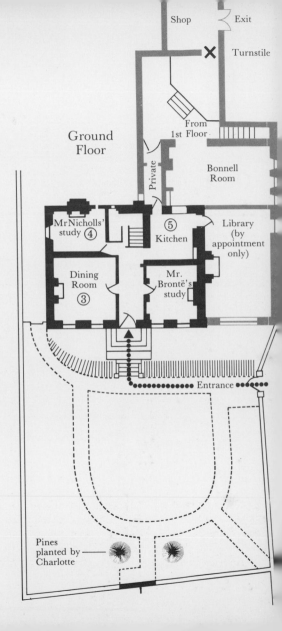

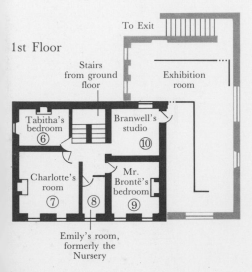

1st Floor

To Exit

Stairs from ground floor

Exhibition room

Tabitha's bedroom ⑥

Branwell's studio ⑩

Charlotte's room ⑦

⑧

Mr. Brontë's bedroom ⑨

Emily's room, formerly the Nursery

■ Walls of the original Brontë Parsonage

■ Post-Brontë additions to the Parsonage

Visitors should now go up the staircase, where a reproduction of Branwell's famous portrait of the Three Sisters hangs. Here also the grandfather clock, which Mr. Brontë used to wind on his way to bed, can be seen.

## 6. Tabitha's Room
This room was originally only entered from the back-yard by an outside stone staircase. Tabitha Aykroyd came to work for the family in 1825 and served them for thirty years. She died in 1855 and is buried beyond the garden wall in front of the Parsonage. Martha Brown came to help at the age of ten and kept house until Mr. Brontë died. This part of the house was altered during the time of the Brontës: the stone mullioned window on the west wall was closed (a trace remains to the right of the fireplace), and the present south window inserted.

## 7. Charlotte's Room
On the right, at the front, is the bedroom in which Mrs. Brontë died in 1821, leaving her small children to be cared for by her sister Elizabeth Branwell. Here Aunt Branwell taught the girls fine needlework and domestic skills. Charlotte's tiny shoes and a dress are displayed with many items which belonged to the sisters and some family china. The garden is seen at its best from these windows.

## 8. Emily's Room, formerly The Nursery
This room was originally larger before Charlotte made her alterations. The children spent many hours here, reading, and writing their juvenile works. Some of the toys displayed were found under the floor during repairs. Emily may have used this room as a bedroom.

## 9. Mr. Brontë's Bedroom
Mr. Brontë used this room after the death of his wife. Some of his possessions are shown. Here he looked after Branwell during his last illness. 'Papa, and sometimes all of us, have sad nights with him,' wrote Charlotte.

## 10. Branwell's Studio
So called because it contains examples of his work as an artist. He had drawing lessons in Keighley and from William Robinson, a Leeds artist of repute. The celebrated portraits of Emily and of the Three Sisters, are in the National Portrait Gallery. Branwell made a little money painting portraits in Bradford for a short time.

## 11. Exhibition Room

This room was added in 1878 and contains items of Brontë interest; special and temporary exhibitions are displayed here together with new acquisitions.

Visitors should now go down the stairs in the exhibition room. At the foot of the stairs turn left into the Bonnell Room.

## 12. The Bonnell Room

This houses the Bonnell Collection of manuscripts and books entrusted to the Brontë Society by the late Henry Houston Bonnell of Philadelphia. Here can be seen many manuscripts and drawings by the Brontës. A published catalogue of the collection is available from Wm. Dawson & Sons Ltd., Cannon House, Folkestone, Kent.

Outside the Bonnell Room is Jocelyn Horner's bronze group which portrays a spiritual interpretation of the Brontë sisters. At the exit there is a shop selling books, postcards and other souvenirs of your visit to the Brontë Parsonage Museum.

## 13. The Garden

Although the layout is essentially the same as it was in the Brontës' day, the garden is at present being replanted with shrubs and flowering plants of the period in an effort to recreate an authentic early Victorian setting for the Parsonage.

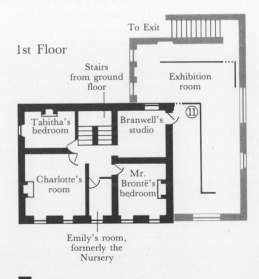

1st Floor

To Exit

Exhibition room

Stairs from ground floor

Tabitha's bedroom

Branwell's studio

⑪

Charlotte's room

Mr. Brontë's bedroom

Emily's room, formerly the Nursery

■ Walls of the original Brontë Parsonage
■ Post-Brontë additions to the Parsonage

## The Library

A comprehensive library is open for research by prior arrangement from Monday to Friday, exclusive of Bank Holidays. Please contact the Librarian/Curator.

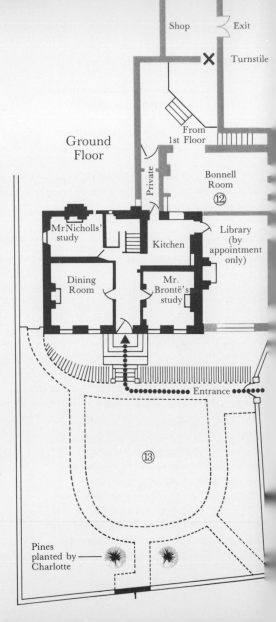

Shop    Exit

✕    Turnstile

From 1st Floor

Ground Floor

Bonnell Room ⑫

Private

Mr Nicholls' study

Kitchen

Library (by appointment only)

Dining Room

Mr. Brontë's study

Entrance

⑬

Pines planted by Charlotte

There is real quality in her references to nature. Such lines as:

> *And wildly through unnumbered trees*
> *The wind of winter sighs*

or

> *How the quiet moonlight sleeps*
> *On this wilderness of snow*

suggest the singleness of vision of the pure in heart. Anne should be placed higher in general estimation as poet and perhaps as novelist.

The Gondal element in Emily's poetry has perhaps been over-emphasised; it is undoubtedly bound up with at least half of the poems, but, even where that element does exist, a poem may well be Gondal and yet reflect a personal experience of Emily's at the same time. The relationship between the dream-world of Gondal and Emily's life as a poet and as a Brontë, is extremely complicated, and I am quite sure that plenty of Emily's real self went into the Gondal poems, though, to be frank, many of the poems which deal most closely with the Gondal myth or saga are frequently melodramatic and not infrequently bad. There is nothing Gondal about the perfect lyric:

> *Fall, leaves, fall; die, flowers, away;*
> *Lengthen night and shorten day;*
> *Every leaf speaks bliss to me,*
> *Fluttering from the autumn tree.*
> *I shall smile when wreaths of snow*
> *Blossom where the rose should grow;*
> *I shall sing when night's decay*
> *Ushers in a drearier day.*

The next poem to this in C. W. Hatfield's 1941 edition of the poems, *is* Gondal certainly, and is, as poetry, very much inferior, but it has good lines, such as:

> *No, that tree with branches riven,*
> *Whitening in the swirl of snow,*
> *As it tossed against the heaven,*
> *Sheltered happy hearts below*

which are marked with that almost magical feeling for nature which is one of the wondrous qualities of Emily's poetry and occasionally of Anne's.

'The Philosopher' is not Gondal, nor the great 'No coward soul is mine,' (printed at the end of this chapter) nor the wonderful poem to the 'God of Visions' (who is the Imagination, but something more). The two famous and beautiful poems, 'Light up thy halls' and 'Cold in the earth' have Gondal attributions but almost certainly they reflect some form of personal experience. The wonderful poem about the blazing sun putting to flight the solemn reign of the stars with its dreams and visions—'Ah; why because the dazzling sun'—is not Gondal, and this poem is a certain sign that Emily had the nature of a mystic and understood the idea of 'the divine Dark', as Vaughan did in his poem '*The Night*' and Novalis, when he wrote his '*Hymns to the Night*'.

It is now clear, certainly, that one of the great mystic passages in Emily's poetry is imbedded in a Gondal poem, much of which is poetically inferior. The six verses in the poem beginning with the line 'He comes with western winds' are some of the most splendid Emily ever wrote, and I am convinced that, surrounded as they are by Gondal verses of little merit, they reveal under a sort of disguise some religious experience (there are no other words for it) of Emily herself. In fact, Emily was not only a romantic poet, but also, I believe, a genuine mystic. This great passage is well known, but it is worth quoting again:

*He comes with western winds, with evening's wandering airs,*
*With that clear dusk of heaven that brings the thickest stars;*
*Winds take a pensive tone, and stars a tender fire,*
*And visions rise and change which kill me with desire—*

*Desire for nothing known in my maturer years*
*When joy grew mad with awe at counting future tears;*
*When, if my spirit's sky was full of flashes warm,*
*I knew not whence they came, from sun or thunderstorm.*

*But first a hush of peace, a soundless calm descends;*
*The struggle of distress and fierce impatience ends;*
*Mute music soothes my breast—unuttered harmony*
*That I could never dream till earth was lost to me.*

*Then dawns the Invisible, the Unseen its truth reveals;*
*My outward sense is gone, my inward essence feels—*
*Its wings are almost free, its home, its harbour found;*
*Measuring the gulf it stoops and dares the final bound!*

*O, dreadful is the check—intense the agony*
*When the ear begins to hear and the eye begins to see;*
*When the pulse begins to throb, the brain to think again,*
*The soul to feel the flesh and the flesh to feel the chain!*

*Yet I would lose no sting, would wish no torture less;*
*The more the anguish racks the earlier it will bless;*
*And robed in fires of Hell, or bright with heavenly shine,*
*If it but herald Death, the vision is divine.*

Charles Morgan has described this passage as '... superb stanzas, the clearest, the most persuasive description of mystical experience in our language'. Whether we agree with this judgment or not, it is clear, at least to me, that this passage is the account not merely of an imagined experience but of a real one.

In one who was both poet and mystic, who shall separate, as Blake would have felt, imagination and reality? But that the Visitant on the western winds, the God of Visions, was a reality to Emily I have no doubt whatever. But Emily was a mystic of Earth, as well as one of Heaven. Put beside the verses just quoted the following:

*The house is old, the trees are bare,*
*And moonless bends the misty dome;*
*But what on earth is half so dear,*
*So longed for as the hearth of home?*

*The mute bird sitting on the stone,*
*The dank moss dripping from the wall,*
*The garden-walk with weeds o'ergrown,*
*I love them—how I love them all;*

There is here an astonishing sense of place, of the immediate, the here and now. The passage is no doubt descriptive of Haworth. Emily loved Haworth not only because there she was in touch with her visions, but also because, it was, what it was in itself.

Two passages in *Wuthering Heights* point the contrast. The first one is:

'And the thing that irks me most is this shattered prison after all. I'm tired of being enclosed here. I'm wearying to escape into that glorious world and to be always there, not seeing it dimly through tears yearning for it through the walls of an aching heart, but really with it and in it . . . I shall be incomparably beyond and above you all'.

And the second:

'I dreamt once that I was in Heaven, Heaven did not seem to be my home; and I broke my heart with weeping to come back to earth; and the angels were so angry that they flung me out into the middle of the heath on the top of Wuthering Heights, where I woke sobbing for joy'.

In this paradox and this contrast is all the mystery of Emily's genius—now rapt in the 'love of the Absolute', and now so close to earth that she seems almost identified with the moss on the wall or with the smallest bell of heather on the boundless moors.

*Diary Fragment written by Emily Brontë on June 26, 1837. Anne and Emily are shown seated writing at the table. (Size 5⅜ × 4⅜ ins.).*

NO COWARD SOUL IS MINE

*No coward soul is mine,*
*No trembler in the world's storm-troubled sphere ;*
*I see Heaven's glories shine*
*And Faith shines equal arming me from Fear.*

*O God within my breast,*
*Almighty ever-present Deity,*
*Life, that in me hast rest*
*As I Undying Life, have power in thee.*

*Vain are the thousand creeds*
*That move men's hearts, unutterably vain,*
*Worthless as withered weeds*
*Or idlest froth amid the boundless main.*

*To waken doubt in one*
*Holding so fast by thy infinity,*
*So surely anchored on*
*The steadfast rock of Immortality.*

*With wide-embracing love*
*Thy spirit animates eternal years,*
*Pervades and broods above,*
*Changes, sustains, dissolves, creates and rears.*

*Though Earth and moon were gone*
*And suns and universes ceased to be*
*And thou were left alone*
*Every existence would exist in thee.*

*There is no room for Death*
*Nor atom that this might could render void,*
*Since Thou art Being and Breath*
*And what Thou art may never be destroyed.*

EMILY JANE BRONTË

*Portrait by P. B. Brontë, now in*
*the National Portrait Gallery,*
*of one of his sisters, variously*
*said to be Emily ( 1818–1848 )*
*and Anne ( 1820–1849 ).*

# The Brontë Parsonage

*Jocelyn Kellett and*
*Donald Hopewell*

The Parsonage was built in 1778. The Brontë family came here from Thornton in 1820 when the children were very young and their mother already in failing health. Basically, the house, built of local stone, is of typical eighteenth century plan; it was modernised by Charlotte when she became a successful writer.

Originally a garden surrounded the house; it was mainly tended by Emily, who planted flowering shrubs and fruit bushes. There was a small backyard containing outbuildings which housed fuel and the family pets. There was an outside privy, now demolished, and also a well. Mr. Brontë kept an account book which records that he paid John Hudson 18/- for painting all windows, doors, gates, water spouts and the water tub.

Letters and diaries of the sisters shed light on the interior decorations of the house; these have proved an invaluable guide when redecoration became necessary. Mrs. Gaskell records that on her visit she found the rooms exquisitely clean with bright fires burning throughout the house.

Charlotte enlarged the dining room and her bedroom above at the expense of the hall, landing and nursery. The nursery was originally wider and was used by Emily as her bedroom. The servants' bedroom and Mr. Nicholls' study were converted from store rooms by Charlotte and the original door casing and stone mullioned window were discovered in recent alterations in Tabitha's room.

Further details of the house, its contents and the way of life of the Brontës can be found in *Haworth Parsonage, the home of the Brontës* (1977) by Jocelyn Kellett.

Mr. Brontë outlived all his children, and after Charlotte died he remained at the Parsonage with her husband. After his death the church and parsonage were much altered to accommodate the new incumbent.

In 1893 the Brontë Society was formed and a small museum set up and housed over the Yorkshire Penny Bank in Haworth. A movement to obtain the Parsonage as a museum was finally successful: in 1928 Haworth-born Sir James Roberts acquired the house and generously gave it to the Society. A little later, now that the Parsonage provided a suitable home for it, Mrs. Helen Safford Bonnell of Philadelphia entrusted to the Society, to be kept together in one room, the wonderful collection of Brontëana made by her late husband, Henry Houston Bonnell, in accordance with his desire, 'he being actuated in large measure by his

*The Parsonage, Haworth, c.1856.*

recognition of the high appreciation of this gifted family by English speaking people on both sides of the Atlantic'. If the gift of the Parsonage brought a new fame to Haworth and an added consequence and importance to the Brontë Society, the coming of the Bonnell Collection made this Yorkshire village the centre of Brontë study and scholarship.

Certain alterations to the Parsonage became essential to meet new functions: the dining room in the north wing became the Society's Library and Council Room, the large bedroom above formed an exhibition gallery, and the remainder of the wing was turned into a house for a caretaker. Unfortunately, it was decided to place the Bonnell Collection in the family dining room, which remained its cramped and unsuitable home for a quarter of a century.

The Council kept in the forefront of their policy the ultimate restoration of the house should funds become available. It needed careful management on a small income before sufficient capital could be accumulated to justify the design; but, at last, the costly work of restoration, including rebuilding and enlargement, was completed with the aid of grants from the Pilgrim Trust and the Museums (Carnegie) Trust, without the need for an appeal to the general public.

The Bonnell Room, exhibition room and a staircase were created from the rear part of the north wing, leading to the shop and exit. Plate glass windows were removed and small panes and glazing bars set in place. None of the new work, carried out in local and weathered stone with old stone roof tiles, is visible from the front of the house.

The kitchen and the family dining room have been restored; the former once again becoming a room (though it must still be used also as a passage and remains without an outside window). The 'fire-spot' has been opened up and now holds a nineteenth century open range from a farm in Ingleton Fells (the gift of Keighley Corporation); a large interior window into the Bonnell Room admits light and provides a pleasing perspective. With the Brontë dresser and cupboard, Emily's baking-tins, and pottery of the period, much of the appearance of Tabby's domain has been recaptured. The dining room is the most complete restoration of all and is especially justified because Mrs. Gaskell gave so clear an account of what it was like when she visited Haworth and because so much of the Brontë furniture which actually stood in it has come back to its former home. A steel and iron grate and marble overmantel, rescued from Methley Hall, recalls the cheerful fireplace that Mrs. Gaskell described, and there are carpet and curtains of a warm crimson colour such as Charlotte introduced. Here hang the engravings of Wellington and Thackeray and a copy of Richmond's portrait of Charlotte, which her publisher sent to Haworth for her pleasure. In the centre of the room is one part of the dining-table round which the sisters used to walk, with the Regency chairs shown in Emily's drawing; and here is the sofa on which Emily died.

In Mr. Brontë's study are drawings of the dogs, and the six Hepplewhite chairs which are the most beautiful pieces of furniture in the whole house. In other rooms are cases displaying dresses, shawls, bonnets and shoes worn by the sisters; there is also the striking 'Apostles Cupboard' so graphically described by Charlotte in *Jane Eyre*.

At the foot of the new staircase is the bronze group (1951) by Jocelyn Horner which, with wonderful technical power, gives a spiritual interpretation of the three sisters; while in an alcove on the old staircase there stands a longcase clock which Mr. Brontë used to wind up on his way to bed. A collection of paintings by Branwell are on view in one of the bedrooms.

The Bonnell Collection is now housed in a large, carefully lit room on the ground floor of the north wing. Here are displayed the drawings, letters, writings and miniature manuscripts of the Brontës, their books and innumerable other possessions.

The furniture displayed in the original part of the house belonged to the Brontës and has been acquired over many years by the Society. Its authenticity is guaranteed by the auctioneer's notebooks, now in the Museum, which give details of the items and names of purchasers at the original sale of the household effects. The Society is happy to see these items restored to their rightful home where they can be seen and enjoyed by everyone.

*Plan of Charlotte's internal alterations to Parsonage, c. 1850.*

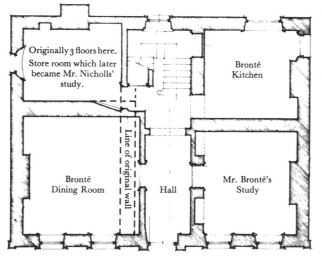

GROUND PLAN

BEDROOM FLOOR

*Immediate right:*
*Diary Fragment. 350 words*
*'November the 24, 1834,*
*Monday. Emily Jane Brontë.*
*I fed Rainbow, Diamond,*
*Snowflake, Jasper . . .' written*
*and signed by Emily Jane Brontë,*
*signed also by Anne Brontë,*
*(2 pp. Size 4 × 2½ ins.,*
*Bonnell Collection, 131).*

*Top far right:*
*HERO, a moorland Merlin Hawk*
*which Emily had as a pet.*
*Watercolour 9⅞ × 8½ ins.,*
*signed and dated 'E. J. Brontë,*
*Oct. 27, 1841'. The Hawk was*
*given away whilst Emily was at*
*school in Brussels. When she*
*returned she 'enquired on all*
*hands and could hear nothing of*
*him'. (Bonnell Collection, 34).*

*Below far right:*
*KEEPER, Emily's dog.*
*Watercolour 5 × 6½ ins., signed*
*and dated 'Keeper from Life,*
*April 24th, 1838. Emily Jane*
*Brontë'.*

# Haworth and its Parish Church

*Ivy Holgate*

Visitors to Haworth frequently ask: at what period does the history of the village commence? The answer must be: in the remote past. Its name in local nomenclature indicates a high farm or settlement. It has no mention in Domesday Book; at the time of the Survey Haworth was a berewick of Bradford manor. A century later only one oxgang (15 acres) was under cultivation. After another century 60 acres had been intaken from the moor and many more freeholders had settled in the district and were engaged in sheep-farming. By 1340 Haworth had become a separate manor and had its own manor court which functioned under succeeding manor lords until 1870. From 1748 to 1870 the court was held at the Kings Arms Inn, later known as the Manor Court House.

The earliest court roll extant is dated 1581. From the rolls we see that Haworth's inhabitants had turbary rights on the moor, and were mainly engaged in farming, the stone quarries and the various textile crafts which were then of a domestic nature. Another glimpse of Haworth in past days is obtained from an Inquisition, dated 1537, on the death of one John Rissheworth: Haworth had then twelve messuages, forty acres of wood, 1,000 acres of waste, 200 acres of pasture and a water mill. Today, one may still see here and there a sturdy, low-built homestead of a yeoman of the 16th or 17th century. There are others beyond the village, while many more have long since disintegrated amid the heather; the small intakes on which they stood have reverted to the moor. During the Civil Wars many dwellings at Haworth were burned to the ground.

At the foot of Old Kirkgate stands the Old Hall, or Emmott Hall, built in Elizabethan days. In its heyday it faced across a green. At the further end of the green was the ducking-stool pond in which the village scolds were ducked. Another relic of old time punishment are the stocks which stand at the foot of the church steps. In bygone days Haworth had its own small prison, also a pinfold for straying cattle. The first half of the 18th century was a period of prosperity and expansion in the worsted industry; many more cottages were built at Haworth alongside the main street and in clusters on its summit. Some of these are distinguished by a third storey with wide windows. These upper rooms were used as weaving chambers and held two or more handlooms.

This rapid increase of dwellings, however, brought evils in its train. These are reflected in the court rolls of Haworth of 1839 and 1843: a dunghill stood beside every cottage; unringed pigs roamed the village, and drinking water was polluted and inadequate for the people's needs. There were frequent outbreaks of typhus, cholera, dysentery and smallpox, and tuberculosis was common. So high was the death rate at Haworth that, in 1850, the General Board of Health instituted an Inquiry. The Report stated that,

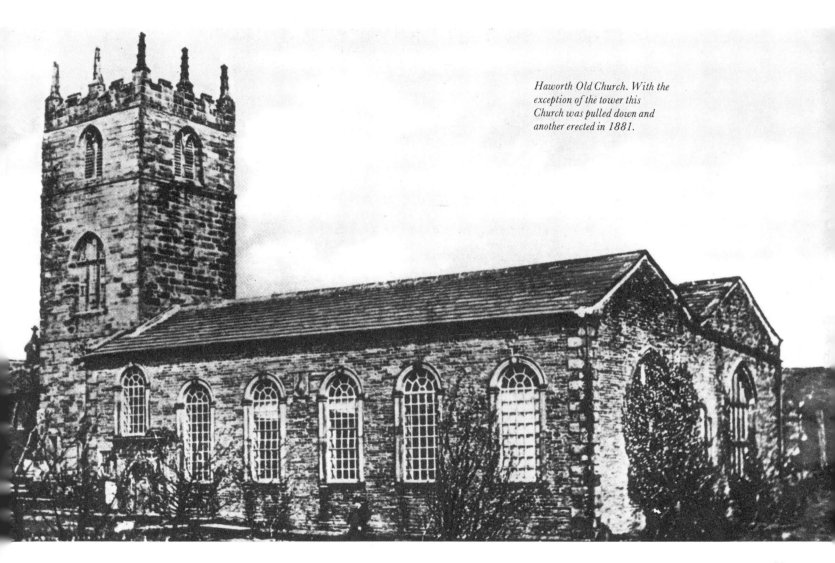

*Haworth Old Church. With the exception of the tower this Church was pulled down and another erected in 1881.*

because of bad sanitation and polluted drinking water, the average age of death was 25.8, while 41.6 per cent of the population died before reaching the age of six years. Under such dreadful conditions it is not surprising that the Brontës, never physically strong, became constant sufferers from a low type of fever which prevailed; this undoubtedly undermined their health and contributed to their untimely deaths. Haworth remained a self-contained village until the coming of the railway. Cut off from cultural centres and softening influences, the people changed little. The inns figured largely in their lives, as did also the annual fairs when drinking, gambling, bloodsports and other vices were indulged in. The steam-powered mills were built in the Victorian period, but in the Brontës' day, the creak of the heavy stone waggons on the cobbles of the hilly street, the clacking of handlooms in all the cottages, and the cry of the plover over the high fields, constituted the pattern and rhythm of everyday life in this moorland village.

The church now standing at Haworth, with the exception of the tower, was built in 1881; it is believed to be the fourth sanctuary to occupy that site. With regard to the earliest structure there has been much conjecture. From the earliest times of which we have record, Haworth has been part of the parish of Bradford, and its earliest chapel would seem to have been contemporary with the first church at Bradford, mention of which occurs in 1281. At this period, and for long afterwards, there existed no place of worship within this extensive parish except the church at Bradford and the chapel at Haworth. In ancient days the stipend of Haworth's curate was contributed by the Vicar of Bradford and the inhabitants of

Haworth, as appears in a monition issued in 1317 from the Ecclesiastical Court at York. In 1338 a Chantry was added to the chapel by the endowment of Richard de Copley. It was probably after the chantries were abolished that the chapel was rebuilt, and the lower portion of the tower of the church is a relic of the ancient chapel which was built prior to the reign of Henry VIII. The tower has been built higher by inserting the middle portion and lifting up the upper portion.

The body of the church was again rebuilt in 1755 by the Reverend William Grimshaw, who was a close friend of John Wesley, and lived in an old house called Sowdens which stands amid the fields, not far from the church. On several occasions John Wesley preached to the people of Haworth and was given hospitality by Grimshaw at Sowdens. Grimshaw's methods of bringing the 'lost sheep' to the fold were unorthodox and often extreme. During the singing of a lengthy hymn, just before the sermon, this zealous parson, armed with his hunting crop, would visit the neighbouring inns and drive the Sabbath breakers into the church. But his methods and his preachings brought so many of Haworth's inhabitants to partake regularly of the Holy Sacrament that it became necessary to provide larger Communion vessels. These pewter flagons are in the keeping of the Rector.

It was in Grimshaw's church the Brontës worshipped. It had a 'three decker' pulpit and pews of black oak, on the doors of which were painted the names of the various freeholds. There were no monuments in the old church. A Brontë memorial was fixed to the east wall after Mr. Brontë's death in 1861. A brass plaque in the church now marks the position of the Brontë vault; it also marks, almost exactly, the spot where stood their pew which they occupied unfailingly every Sabbath. The Church register transcripts at York date back to 1600. Those at Haworth Church commence in the year 1645, and contain much interesting data which reflects the customs and habits of the people of the parish in bygone days. Over the chancel arch there is a striking fresco of a Calvary. On the south side is a stained glass window given by an American citizen to the memory of Charlotte Brontë.

Another monument of interest is the memorial to the Reverend William Weightman who was for three years Curate at Haworth and was nicknamed 'Celia Amelia' by the Brontë sisters. In a glass case are exhibited a Cambridge folio Bible dated 1659, and the Certificate of Marriage between Charlotte Brontë and the Reverend Arthur Bell Nicholls.

The Brontë Memorial Chapel is the most recent addition to the church; it occupies the previously redundant south-east portion. At its entrance stand two tall stone pillars, each one carrying an inscription. That on the left gives the information that, at its base, beneath the pavement, the Brontë vault is situated in which lie the remains of the Brontë family, with the exception of Anne who died and was buried at Scarborough. The inscription on the right-hand pillar records that the Chapel was the gift of Sir Tresham Lever and was dedicated by the Bishop of Bradford on July 4, 1964. The Brontë Memorial Chapel, though only recently constructed, blends perfectly with the older fabric of the church; the work has been carried out with thoughtful care by local craftsmen. The pews are contemporary with those in the nave of the church. The screen at the entrance to the Chapel is of oak, the design based on that of the older screen of the chancel.

By a pleasing coincidence, certain relics which once had a place in Mr. Brontë's church have been brought back after many years and can now be seen in the Chapel. A 17th century table of carved oak occupies the central position below a stained glass window; it was before this table, used for the Holy Sacrament in Mr. Brontë's day, that Charlotte and the Rev. A. B. Nicholls would kneel to be joined together in wedlock. Another interesting item is the fine candelabra. This bears an inscription on its base which tells that it was introduced into Haworth Church by the Rev. William Grimshaw when he rebuilt the church during the 18th century. It was taken to Hubberholme when the church was again rebuilt in 1879, where it remained until 1964. A brass wall plaque with branching candlesticks, which also belonged to the church in the Brontës' day, has been presented by a London lady.

On the south wall is the plaque recording the births and deaths of Mr. and Mrs. Brontë and all their children; opposite this is a small plaque in memory of Elizabeth Branwell, Mrs. Brontë's sister, who took charge of the children after the death of their mother and devoted the rest of her life to their care.

The Brontë Memorial Chapel is a tranquil place where those visiting Haworth can rest and meditate on the genius and courage of three sisters who lived quietly and simply in this moorland village.

# The Brontë Society

*Edith Weir*

The Brontë Society which administers the Parsonage, is the doyen of English literary societies. Founded in 1893 it has a length of life unchallenged by any contemporary or earlier society. Only the Dickens Fellowship, founded in 1902, is of similar age and vitality. Of those that have come and gone the longest lived was the Chaucer Society, which lasted just under thirty years. Two successive Shakespeare Societies did not between them total more than thirty years. After six years the work of the Wordsworth Society, attracting by then the enthusiastic efforts of only two committee men, came to an end. The Browning Society, like the Dickens Fellowship, had its counterparts in local groups all over the country, and though some of these may have outlived by a few years the original one, this lasted only from 1881 to 1893.

But the Brontë Society goes on from strength to strength. Its members are spread all over the world. The American membership is so large that it was found expedient to have an Honorary American Representative, and it was the proud achievement of the first Representative, Helen Arnold, to secure members from all of the American States. Notable libraries of the world are subscribing members of the Society.

What is there in the Brontë Society to account for its survival, let alone its continued growth? Its unique

position is not explained by the bland axiom that nothing succeeds like success, for it has had its periods of setbacks and discouragement. But the only suggestion that it should end its activities came from, of all people, Clement Shorter, who in 1914 wrote to suggest that it should be wound up. The Society's minutes record, with what must have been remarkable restraint and under-statement, that 'the members present failed to agree with Mr. Shorter'.

The Society was first suggested, where it has so often since been sustained and encouraged, in the columns of the Yorkshire press. A journalist, W. W. Yates, who had been interested in the Dewsbury associations of the Brontës, wrote to the *Dewsbury Reporter* of November 22, 1893, and also to the *Leeds Mercury Weekly Supplement*, the *Bradford Observer*, *Keighley News* and *Halifax Guardian* letters suggesting that the time had arrived when an effort should be made to secure and to preserve for the use of the public for ever the literary and other relics of the Brontë sisters. 'Little by little', he wrote, 'through the researches of this person or that, we have learned more and more of the Brontës, and, on the other hand, their one-time belongings are becoming more and more scattered, if they are not also becoming fewer in number; and unless a systematic effort be soon made to gather them together I fear the carrying out of a scheme for a museum will become impossible . . . A necessary preliminary to all this is the establishment of a Brontë Society . . .'

In the following issue of the *Mercury Weekly Supplement* J. H. Erskine-Stuart of Heckmondwike wrote: 'All that Mr. W. W. Yates has said on the subject of the proposed Brontë Society is very much to the point, but I am afraid the first scheme (the museum) can only be carried out in a very imperfect manner'.

But before his rather discouraging note had been sounded the enthusiasts had rallied, Mr. Yates's suggestion had won support from all over the country; he was invited to put his ideas before Sir John Brigg and a few friends in Bradford. Less than three weeks after the first suggestion the Mayor of Bradford, Alderman Jonas Whitley, had sent out a circular to interested people calling them to a meeting at the Town Hall on December 16. More than fifty people were there and many encouraging letters and messages were read, including one from George Smith, Charlotte Brontë's publisher.

The Rev. W. H. Keeling, Headmaster of Bradford Grammar School, presided in the absence of the Mayor. His case for a Brontë Society was simple, direct and free from any intimidating suggestion of an exclusive literary cult. The Brontës, he said, though not Yorkshire themselves, thoroughly represented the spirit of the county in their deep and tender feelings, in their trenchant manner of speech, and in their detestation of all that was weak and undesirable. In the delineation of Yorkshire character and the representation of Yorkshire scenery they formed the strongest link between the county and the great world of literature. He considered that those present ought to be proud that the neighbourhood was connected with so great a family and ought to adopt reasonable means to perpetuate their association.

If nothing else could have roused their support, this well-directed appeal to regional pride could not fail to win the West Riding gathering. A society was formed and a Council elected. Sir John Brigg became Chairman of the Council, Lord Houghton (later the Marquess of Crewe) accepted the Presidency, and Sir Thomas Wemyss Reid, Augustine Birrell and George Smith were among the vice-presidents.

At the second Council meeting it was reported that a collection of Brontë relics was on sale for £500, but this figure was far beyond a society scarcely on its feet. Much more in keeping with its modest status was the gift from Dents, the publishers, of a set of Brontë works, and the purchase of the Brontë sofa for £5. Then Routledges, the publishers, sent a set of Brontë novels.

A special Museum Fund was created for the purpose of securing important relics which could only be obtained by purchase. Looking back now on the small fortunes that have changed hands for Brontë treasures and on the considerable sums spent by the Society itself, one feels it was as well for the peace of mind and continuing efforts of those members of 1894 that they could record confidently that '£300 will be sufficient to purchase all the relics worth preserving, and, as several gifts of Brontë relics and books are to hand or have been promised, it may be assumed that very little expenditure in this direction will be necessary in the future'.

The response to the Museum Fund appeal was not encouraging and early purchases were in no way spectacular. But an increasing number of relics began to arrive as gifts, and progress generally was regarded as satisfactory. At the end of its first year the Society had 170 members and £29 in hand. Among its acquisitions were a photograph of Patrick Brontë, the first of the two circulars it now owns—the only ones known to exist—of the proposed 'The Misses Brontë's Establishment for the Board and Education of a Limited Number of Young Ladies', and a large oil painting by Branwell, presented by Mr. William Law, of Honresfeld. He offered other relics, letters and pictures on loan, and the Society decided the time had come for a Museum. It secured a room over the Yorkshire Penny Bank at Haworth.

Today it is surprising to discover that the decision to have the Museum at Haworth was not a foregone conclusion. The claims of Dewsbury and Bradford were urged by some members, who felt that Haworth was too remote. Indeed, at the meeting at which the decision was taken the Haworth members had to leave to catch their train before the voting, which decided on the small moorland town by only six to four.

The little museum was opened by Sir John Brigg on May 18, 1895. The Midland Railway ran a special train, flags were flying, a band was playing, and the sun, after a grey morning, flooded the afternoon scene while the crowds climbed the steep hill to the Museum with its little bust of Thackeray set in the centre of the window. During the summer Smith, Elder and Co. sent on loan the manuscripts of *Jane Eyre* and *Villette*, and in seven months the museum attracted nearly 10,000 visitors. One of these was Charlotte's friend, Ellen Nussey, and the records suggest that under her close scrutiny the exhibits revealed only one flaw : a portrait by Charlotte was not of Emily, as stated, but of Anne.

There was a most conscientious effort to keep the museum accurate and authentic, and in this respect the Society's poverty was almost an asset. It could not indulge in the luxury of buying anything not known to be genuine. Fortunately there were still people living whose first-hand knowledge of the Brontës could be sought. When a portrait of Anne was offered, it was submitted to the Rev. A. B. Nicholls, Charlotte's husband, in Ireland, and he at once denounced it as a fraud.

The Society was, however, and always has been, much more than a managing body for a museum. In January 1895 the first publication was issued : Butler Wood's 'Bibliography of the Works of the Brontë Family', an invaluable source of reference to those embarking on a close study of the Brontës and one that he supplemented two years later. Other publications were 'Haworth, Home of the Brontës', and 'A Chronology of the Principal Events in the Lives of the Brontës'. Some of the early publications point to the intense interest that has always existed in the places and people of the Brontë novels. In many ways it was an interest that had been over-indulged : in their efforts to identify originals the zealots had wandered on to many doubtful paths. But there was no ignoring the extent of the interest, and the Society's efforts to establish reasonable accuracy culminated in that invaluable guide to the Brontë pilgrim, Herbert Wroot's 'Persons and Places in the Novels of Charlotte Brontë'.

An annual excursion was a natural and popular offshoot of this interest, and this and the annual meeting brought together each year members in the North Country and always some enthusiasts from far away. For those who could take no direct part in these activities the Annual *Transactions* served as the main link. In his editor's preface to the 1899 *Transactions* Butler Wood wrote: 'It will be noticed that the contributions are more literary and less biographical or topographical in character than formerly . . . It is not only desirable but necessary that the Society should devote more attention to the literary aspects of the Brontë writings than it has attempted hitherto'.

From that time onwards the *Transactions* have been a publication that no serious Brontë student could dispense with. Not only have they contained the stimulating appreciation of those who addressed the Society's meetings but they have offered guidance in the controversies always springing up and exciting glimpses of that land so full of promise, the unpublished and juvenile writings of the Brontës.

An outstanding contributor from 1920 until his death in 1942 was C. W. Hatfield. He was the first person to master the task of deciphering the cryptic writing of Emily Brontë—a skill which enabled him eventually to produce the first complete collection of her poems. The result of those of his researches which appeared in the *Transactions* raised the status of that publication, and with it that of the Society, to a position of even

securer authority. In all matters relating to the Brontës he was almost religiously accurate. 'It is better to leave possibilities out of the question and to allow probabilities to have only small weight', he once wrote. 'Both of these are apt to lead one astray. It is evidence that counts'. He set an example in research which inspired other members, so that there were more and more contributions by those who, patiently and absorbedly followed their own special lines of research and criticism.

In the early 1920s, with total funds of £170 and a then record membership of 270, the Society was far from permanently secure and was nowhere near its ambition of buying Haworth Parsonage, or, indeed of being able to pay the prices that were being asked for Brontë relics and manuscripts as they came on the market. But it was established on a firm foundation of scholarship, integrity and good husbandry. Its reputation had spread thousands of miles beyond the cluster of West Riding towns from which it drew its governing members. People had confidence in its guardianship of Brontë treasures and Brontë traditions. In the sale rooms wealthy collectors could always outbid the Society and this often meant that not only Haworth, but England, lost the literary treasures that belonged to her, so more and more people sent their Brontë souvenirs to Haworth as gifts.

The Society received its accolade when an American collector, Henry Houston Bonnell, of Philadelphia, signified his intention of bequeathing to it his Brontëana—the finest single collection in the world of manuscripts and drawings. The full significance of this decision is often overlooked today when the Society is sturdy and prosperous and securely housed at the Parsonage, but to miss its import is to miss one of those small miracles that make life exciting. Mr. Bonnell's collection had been gathered with intense care and at much cost. It was one of the joys of his life. He wanted it to remain intact and cherished after his death. Any of the famous libraries of the world would have gladly opened their doors to it and housed it with supreme pride. But he chose as its guardian the little Society, with a one-room museum and 270 members, who had been inspired to perpetuate the Brontë memory. Those who care that England shall preserve her treasures of literature will never forget Mr. Bonnell's superb gift. But they should also never forget what they owe to that handful of obscure enthusiasts whose devoted work not only held the Society together in times of difficulty but endowed it with the character and repute that made it eligible for such a gift.

The promise of the Bonnell Collection intensified the longing to acquire the Parsonage. This part of the story, too, has an exciting quality. At the Annual Meeting in 1927, when the entire cash assets of the Society were just under £50, it was reported that the Haworth Church Lands Trustees were prepared to consider selling the Parsonage for about £3,000. Somebody posted a newspaper report of this meeting to Sir James Roberts, who was abroad at the time. Lady Roberts, on being shown the cutting, suggested to her husband that this was his chance to do something for his native Haworth. Sir James offered not only to buy the Parsonage but to contribute £1,500 towards the cost of fitting it up as a museum. On August 4, 1928, the Brontë Parsonage was opened as a Museum and Library. It was sixty-seven years since the last of the

Brontës had followed his children to the grave in Haworth Church, and now their home received them again. There were tears as Sir James described his presentation of the title deeds to the Society as an act of homage to the genius, nobility and courage of the three sisters.

The Society now entered a new phase of its life, for with the Bonnell Collection, to reach Haworth later in the year, the Parsonage became one of the nations' finest literary memorials. Conscious of its new responsibilities the Council invited the Universities of Oxford, Cambridge, Leeds and Sheffield, and certain local bodies to appoint representatives.

Attendances at the Parsonage boomed for some years, but then came the war. In 1940 the Society's income no longer covered current expenditure, and the modest reserves were drawn upon. For four years the situation was an anxious one. Then in 1944 the position changed excitingly. Membership moved quickly from an apparently static 400, and visitors to the Parsonage for the year reached more than 20,000— more than double any previous figure. Membership has gone up every year since; in 1969 visitors numbered 100,000, and five years later had passed the 200,000 mark.

The genius of the Brontës received England's seal when in 1944 the Society's memorial to the sisters took its place in the Poets' Corner at Westminster Abbey. The renewed interest in the Brontës was only faintly stirring in that year, but by 1947, when the memorial was formally handed over by the Society at a service in July it had swept the Brontës to new heights of fame and acclaimed their right to be among the great names of English literature.

What is the Society's task now that the Brontë memory is preserved at Haworth and at the national shrine at Westminster? It continues to steer a path through the fog of legend that is always in danger of obscuring the Brontë story, to sustain enthusiasm with constant research and new critical approach, to restore to the Parsonage more of the possessions of the Brontës, and to preserve for new generations the resources for what will always be a fascinating study in literary history. Dare one apply the final and searching question, beloved of those who are cynical about literary societies? — How would the Brontës themselves regard the Brontë Society? The dangers in the question dissolve if we use a simpler form of questioning: Would the sincere and unpretentious efforts to honour their memory affront the Brontës! Would their shy, home-loving natures find anything forbiddingly alien in the kindly, unassuming folk, always predominantly West Yorkshire, who have shaped and directed the Society? Would they not follow with surprised pleasure the many threads connecting members of today with their own days at Haworth? Though each sister, with the humility of the true artist, would disclaim the honour for herself, would she not feel proud and delighted that it was accorded to the others?

*1928 street scene of Haworth — showing opening of Parsonage.*
*See* Brontë Society Transactions **7**: *137–150 (1928).*

# The Brontë Society Transactions

*Charles H. Lemon*

The Society's *Transactions* have appeared annually since 1895. In the early years there was inevitably some emphasis on personal reminiscences, bibliography and topography but as time went on interest shifted to a re-assessment of the Brontës and of their place in literature as novelists and poets. Since the publication of Mrs. Gaskell's *Life* many books about them had appeared but the early reviews of their works were largely forgotten. A change of emphasis is reflected in the Addresses delivered at the Society's Annual Public Meetings. These Addresses, given by famous literary figures, leading academics, clerics and social historians, have been published in *Transactions* since their inception.

One unchanging feature of *Transactions* of great interest down the years has been the printing of Brontë letters, drawings and manuscripts, some previously unpublished, which have in many cases been acquired by the Society. For example, Charlotte's letters to M. Heger, written after her return from Brussels and now in the British Museum, were printed in the issue for 1914, and in 1925 several of Branwell's letters, illustrated by his own sketches, were published. Charlotte's writing desk and its contents were featured in 1944, shortly after it had come into the possession of the Society. A facsimile of Emily's diary paper of 26th June 1837 and a transcription were printed in the issue for 1951. In 1958 an illustrated article was published about Branwell's portrait of his sisters, now in the National Portrait Gallery, reporting that after examination a fourth figure had been traced, probably that of Branwell himself, which had been painted out. Fragments of unpublished novels by Charlotte were published in 1899 and 1936. More recently Charlotte's preface to *Shirley* written in reply to the harsh review of *Jane Eyre* which appeared in *The Quarterly* has been published. Her publisher declined to use it and it remained unknown for well over a century until printed in *Transactions*.

The past twenty-five years have seen a steady output of books about the Brontës and it has been satisfactory to note the use which their authors have made of material published in *Transactions*. On the other hand it is remarkable that after over eighty years there is still no lack of manuscripts submitted, and unquestionably the distinction of having work accepted by the Society for publication is much valued. A published index, compiled by Amy G. Foster, to volumes 1–15 (1895–1967 inclusive) of the *Transactions* is available from the Society.

The many parts of *Transactions* have now become collectors' items but they are at the same time indispensable to researchers and students, and a source of fascinating interest for the general reader.

*Above:*
*Title-page (2×1⅜ ins.) of Charlotte Brontë's manuscript (dated 28th June 1830),* The Evening Walk, *purchased by the Brontë Society in 1972; see* Brontë Society Transactions **16**: 110–112 (1972).

*Left:*
*Fragment (¾×4¼ ins.) of Napolean's coffin bearing inscription by M. Lebel, and accompanying note (dated 4th August 1843) by Charlotte Brontë purchased by the Brontë Society in 1978; see* Brontë Society Transactions **17**: 185–188 (1978).

## Contributors

Sir W. Linton Andrews, LL.D., D.Litt. (d. 1972)
Journalist and writer; editor of the *Yorkshire Post;*
Chairman of the Brontë Society Council.

Juliet R. V. Barker, M.A., D.Phil.
Curator and Librarian, Brontë Parsonage Museum.

Phyllis Bentley, O.B.E., D.Litt. (d. 1977)
Novelist and Brontë biographer;
Brontë Society Council member.

Wilfred Rowland Childe, M.A. (d. 1952)
Poet and Senior Lecturer in English Literature,
University of Leeds; Brontë Society Council member.

Donald G. Hopewell, M.A., LL.D. (d. 1983)
Brontë Society Council member;
President of the Brontë Society.

Ivy Holgate (d. 1976)
Writer and local historian;
Brontë Society Council member.

Jocelyn E. Kellett, B.Com.
President of the Brontë Society.

Charles H. Lemon
Former Editor of the Brontë Society *Transactions.*

Edith M. Weir
Vice-President and former Secretary of the Brontë Society.

## The Brontë Society

Full details of membership of the Society, together
with information on its publications, excursions,
lecture services and research facilities, can be obtained
from the Hon. Correspondence Secretary, c/o the
Brontë Parsonage, Haworth, Keighley, West
Yorkshire BD22 8DR. (Tel: Haworth (0535) 42323).

Membership offers the following advantages:-

● Free admission to the Parsonage

● Free access to Library (by prior arrangement)

● Annual *Transactions*

● Literary Luncheons

● Excursions to places of Brontë interest.

● Addresses by Eminent Speakers

● Temporary Exhibitions